# travel journal

MW01489778

## if found,
## please return to:

.......................................................................................

*Name*

.......................................................................................

*Address*

.......................................................................................

*Phone*

.......................................................................................

*Email*

# I really want to see:

# My travel itinerary:

# Things to do before the trip:

- ☐ VACCINATIONS
- ☐ APPLY FOR VISA
- ☐ BOOK A FLIGHT
- ☐ BOOK ACCOMMODATION
- ☐ BOOK A RENTAL CAR
- ☐ TRAVEL INSURANCE
- ☐ CHECK CREDIT CARD
- ☐ CHECK BANK ACCOUNT
- ☐ COPY OF IMPORTANT DOCUMENTS ONLINE
- ☐ BUS / TRAIN TICKETS BOOKING
- ☐ CHECK PASSPORT
- ☐ TRAVEL PLAN FOR FRIENDS / FAMILY
- ☐ BURGLARY PROTECTION
- ☐
- ☐
- ☐
- ☐
- ☐
- ☐
- ☐
- ☐
- ☐
- ☐
- ☐
- ☐
- ☐
- ☐

# My packing list:

## Bath & Body

☐
☐
☐
☐
☐
☐
☐
☐
☐
☐
☐
☐
☐
☐
☐
☐
☐

## Clothing

☐
☐
☐
☐
☐
☐
☐
☐
☐
☐
☐
☐
☐
☐
☐
☐
☐
☐
☐
☐
☐
☐
☐
☐
☐
☐
☐
☐

## MISCELLANEOUS

☐
☐
☐
☐
☐
☐
☐
☐
☐
☐
☐
☐
☐
☐
☐
☐
☐
☐

## Electric / photo

☐
☐
☐
☐
☐
☐
☐
☐
☐
☐
☐
☐
☐
☐

## CARRY-ON BAGGAGE

☐ Visa/Passport
☐ Creditcard
☐ Cash
☐ Flight / bus / train tickets
☐ Travel documents
☐ Hygiene
☐ Camera, batteries
☐ Mobile phone, charger
☐ Headphone
☐ Travel journal
☐
☐
☐
☐
☐

Date:_____     Place:_____

Date:_____ Place:_____

Date:_____          Place:_____

Date:_____     Place:_____

Date:_____  Place:_____

Date:_____    Place:_____

Date:_____     Place:_____

Date:_____     Place:_____

Date:_____     Place:_____

Date:_____    Place:_____

Date:_____     Place:_____

Date:_____     Place:_____

Date:_____     Place:_____

Date:_____          Place:_____

Date:_____     Place:_____

Date:_____     Place:_____

Date:_____          Place:_____

**Date:**_____     **Place:**_____

Date:_____     Place:_____

Date:_____  Place:_____

Date:_____ Place:_____

Date:_____     Place:_____

Date:_____     Place:_____

Date:_____ Place:_____

Date:_____ Place:_____

Date:_____ Place:_____

Date:_____     Place:_____

Date:_____     Place:_____

**Date:**_____    **Place:**_____

Date:_____          Place:_____

Date:_____     Place:_____

Date:_____   Place:_____

Date:_____     Place:_____

Date:_____   Place:_____

Date:_____    Place:_____

Date:_____          Place:_____

Date: _____   Place: _____

Date:_____ Place:_____

Date:_____  Place:_____

_____

_____

_____

_____

_____

_____

_____

_____

_____

_____

_____

_____

_____

_____

_____

_____

_____

_____

_____

_____

_____

_____

_____

_____

_____

_____

_____

_____

Date:_____ Place:_____

# This travel experience will always affect me:

My very favorite photo

# I take that important experience from my trip with:

# Next time I plan to do:

_____

_____

_____

_____

_____

_____

_____

_____

_____

_____

_____

_____

_____

_____

_____

_____

_____

_____

_____

_____

_____

_____

# Contacts of acquaintances:

NAME:
WHERE MET:
PHONE:
EMAIL:

NAME:
WHERE MET:
PHONE:
EMAIL:

NAME:
WHERE MET:
PHONE:
EMAIL:

NAME:
WHERE MET:
PHONE:
EMAIL:

NAME:
WHERE MET:
PHONE:
EMAIL:

NAME:
WHERE MET:
PHONE:
EMAIL:

NAME:
WHERE MET:
PHONE:
EMAIL:

NAME:
WHERE MET:
PHONE:
EMAIL:

# Contacts of acquaintances:

NAME:
WHERE MET:
PHONE:
EMAIL:

NAME:
WHERE MET:
PHONE:
EMAIL:

NAME:
WHERE MET:
PHONE:
EMAIL:

NAME:
WHERE MET:
PHONE:
EMAIL:

NAME:
WHERE MET:
PHONE:
EMAIL:

NAME:
WHERE MET:
PHONE:
EMAIL:

NAME:
WHERE MET:
PHONE:
EMAIL:

NAME:
WHERE MET:
PHONE:
EMAIL:

# NOTES:

# NOTES:

# NOTES:

# NOTES:

# NOTES:

# NOTES:

# NOTES:

# NOTES:

# NOTES:

# NOTES:

NOTES, PHOTOS, TICKETS, SOUVENIRS

# Notes, photos, tickets, souvenirs

# NOTES, PHOTOS, TICKETS, SOUVENIRS

# Notes, photos, tickets, souvenirs

# Notes, photos, tickets, souvenirs

Made in the USA
San Bernardino, CA
11 December 2019